Tate Gallery St Ives

Introduction

Since the late nineteenth century two 'schools' of
art have grown up in west Cornwall, at Newlyn and
St Ives. Newlyn school painting is displayed at the
public gallery in Penzance, but before the Tate
Gallery St Ives opened in 1993, there had been no
similar arrangement for the distinctive modern art
of St Ives. The Tate Gallery St Ives presents
twentieth-century art in the context of Cornwall.
At the heart of its programme of displays and
activities is a body of work for which the town of
St Ives is internationally known, the modernist art
produced by artists associated with the town and
its surrounding area from the 1920s onwards. The
Gallery also presents new work made by younger
artists, responding to the Gallery's displays or to
the broader Cornish scene. The Barbara Hepworth
Museum and Sculpture Garden opened in 1976 and
is now part of the Tate Gallery St Ives.

The Tate Gallery continues to acquire work for
its collections, and remains committed to showing
works associated with Cornwall in both London
and Liverpool as well as in St Ives. Moreover, the
links between the arts and artists of west Cornwall
and other centres around the world mean that
the Tate Gallery St Ives also displays related works
by non-Cornish artists.

A Visit to Tate St Ives

The Tate Gallery St Ives presents modern art created in or associated with Cornwall. The building was specifically designed to house this work. Its location in St Ives, with dramatic views across the town and harbour to the east and Porthmeor Beach to the north, provides a unique opportunity to view the work in the surroundings in which, in many cases, it was actually created.

Visiting the galleries

The displays in the Tate St Ives regularly change, with a major rehang of all the galleries taking place once a year in the autumn (the galleries are closed for two weeks at this time). This allows a different selection from the Tate Gallery's extensive collection of St Ives art to be shown each year, offering a variety of ways in which the 'St Ives school' can be appreciated. In addition, there are temporary exhibitions focusing on a particular artist or theme. Through its programme of artists' projects, the Gallery encourages and enables the creation of new work relating to the local environment.

The displays begin in the first room, the Mall, which contains a large coloured glass window designed by Patrick Heron. They continue in the Rotunda from where stairs lead up to the bookshop on the first floor and to the second floor Information Desk and gallery area (access to all floors can also be gained via a lift to the right of the Rotunda). To the left of the Information Desk, Gallery 1 displays work from the earlier period of St Ives art from around 1900 to the 1940s. Gallery 2 is on two levels and affords a panoramic view of Porthmeor Beach. The upper level contains a large curved show-case devoted to ceramics associated with the potter Bernard Leach (see p.26). The lower level or Lower Terrace displays larger paintings (mostly landscapes from the period after 1945) and sculpture, and gives access to the education studio where there are changing exhibitions of work produced as a result of educational activities. Returning to the upper level, Gallery 3 is used for special exhibitions, and Galleries 4 and 5 display work from the 1950s to the present. A small open-air garden, accessible from the second floor and by steps down from the roof terrace, is used for temporary displays of sculpture by artists in residence. The café on the top floor acts as an occasional display area for special projects and work by community-based groups, and contemporary ceramics can also be seen here and at other points throughout the building.

Ceramics displays
at the Tate Gallery
St Ives

Tours and talks

The Tate St Ives runs a comprehensive outreach and education programme, including tours, workshops, talks and other events. Details of exhibitions and events can be found in a separate leaflet available at the Information Desk.

Café and shop

The café is situated on the fourth floor. The shop is situated on the first floor. A wide range of books and gifts is available.

Patrick Heron *Window for Tate Gallery St Ives* 1992–3

Opposite left A view of the town and island from the Gallery

Opposite right Inside the Gallery: the Lower Terrace, Gallery 2

The Building

The Tate Gallery St Ives opened in 1993. It occupies the site of a former gasworks on the northern edge of the 'downalong' district of St Ives, the heart of the town's traditional fishing community. (By contrast, the 'upalong' district grew up on the higher slopes of the town from the late nineteenth century, providing spacious terraced housing for the more prosperous families and the growing number of tourists.)

The architects Eldred Evans and David Shalev have described themselves as 'single-minded modernists with the conviction that a building, built to last, is rooted in time and place'. For the gallery they adopted two basic forms that echo those on the original site: a cylinder, recalling the old gas-holder, and a steep-sided rectangular form that relates to earlier post-war buildings along Porthmeor Beach. Some important themes in their design can be appreciated as you pass through the building. These include the relationship between the interior space and views of the landscape and sea outside; the experience of geometric forms and spaces brought to life by different qualities of light, colour and surface; and echoes of the topography of St Ives itself, with its network of streets, small squares and steep alleys.

When the Gallery is approached from the harbour area of St Ives, the first view of it from Back Road West suggests a building growing naturally out of the clusters of houses around it. The Porthmeor Beach elevation and the interior detailing, however, reflect the modernist tradition that is central to the art of St Ives, with the use of interrelated geometric forms, white walls and simple wood and slate finishes. In the architects' words, 'The experience of visiting the Gallery ought to be a natural extension of visiting St Ives and thus provide some insight into the artists' inspirations and aspirations on this remote and magical island'.

Gallery 2 Lower Terrace

Left The view from Porthmeor Beach

Right The gasworks, Porthmeor Beach *c.*1963

The Barbara Hepworth Studio and Sculpture Garden

Barbara Hepworth first came to live in Cornwall with her husband Ben Nicholson and their young family at the outbreak of war in 1939. From 1949 she worked in Trewyn Studio, which from about 1950 also became her home. She died in 1975, and, following her wish to establish her home and studio as a museum of her work, in 1980 Trewyn Studio and much of the artist's work remaining there was given to the nation and placed in the care of the Tate Gallery.

'Finding Trewyn Studio was a sort of magic', wrote Barbara Hepworth; 'here was a studio, a yard and garden where I could work in open air and space'. When she first arrived at Trewyn Studio, Hepworth was still largely preoccupied with stone and wood carving, but during the 1950s she increasingly made sculpture in bronze as well. This led her to create works on a more monumental scale, for which she

Barbara Hepworth *Single Form (September)* 1961

Above and opposite Two views of the Sculpture Garden

used the garden as a viewing area. The bronzes now in the garden are seen in the environment for which they were created, and most are in the positions in which the artist herself placed them. The garden itself was laid out by Barbara Hepworth with help from a friend, the composer Priaulx Rainier.

The museum and garden give a powerful and moving impression of the way Barbara Hepworth worked while living in St Ives.

What is St Ives Art?

Artists have been coming to work in St Ives since the nineteenth century. From the 1880s onwards, Newlyn, St Ives and the west Cornwall hinterland were firmly on the map as destinations for artists seeking a quasi-communal way of living and working – on the lines of the continental art colony of Pont-Aven in Brittany – as well as fresh subject matter in the landscape, climate and social realities of this still-remote area of the country.

For more than a century there have been many artists producing realistically observed marine and landscape paintings in a tradition little altered from that established by the Newlyn school. St Ives' place in art history, however, is most firmly identified with a very different kind of art, produced by painters and sculptors working in the modernist tradition and its later offshoots. The term 'St Ives school' has been loosely applied to the succession of painters and sculptors active in west Cornwall from the 1940s onwards, who explored the potential of abstract art and, later, strove to combine abstract formal language with landscape themes and subjects.

The association of St Ives with avant-garde artists began as early as 1925, when Cedric Morris stayed in the town. The paintings he made there were seen by Christopher Wood, who visited St Ives in 1926 and two years later returned in the company of Ben Nicholson. On this visit, in August 1928, the cosmopolitan Wood and Nicholson 'discovered' the self-taught mariner-painter Alfred Wallis, whose work soon attracted attention in sophisticated artistic circles and was profoundly to influence Nicholson in particular. Modernism became firmly established in St Ives during the Second World War, when Nicholson and Barbara Hepworth settled there, attracting a circle of other modernist artists such as Naum Gabo. These artists shared an intellectual and aesthetic outlook that was essentially European rather than insular, but the work they produced in St Ives was nevertheless often deeply influenced by the physical forms and quality of light of their local surroundings.

Many of the artists whose names are linked with St Ives have been incomers who have chosen west

Stanhope Forbes
The Health of the Bride
1889

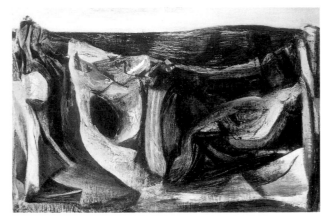

Above Alfred Wallis '*The Hold House Port Mear Square Island Port Mear Beach*' ?*c.*1932

Above right Christopher Wood *Boat in Harbour, Brittany* 1929

Right Peter Lanyon *Headland* 1948

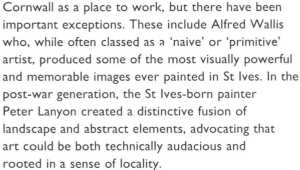

Cornwall as a place to work, but there have been important exceptions. These include Alfred Wallis who, while often classed as a 'naive' or 'primitive' artist, produced some of the most visually powerful and memorable images ever painted in St Ives. In the post-war generation, the St Ives-born painter Peter Lanyon created a distinctive fusion of landscape and abstract elements, advocating that art could be both technically audacious and rooted in a sense of locality.

Nor is art in St Ives simply the story of a succession of talented individual artists who happen to have worked here. The activities of artistic groups and societies, the concentration of studios and galleries in the town, and the active teaching of varieties of art practice have combined both to reinforce a distinctive tradition and to generate new works and ideas.

Below right Naum Gabo *Circular Relief c.*1925

From Celts to Colonists: Before 1920

Viewed as a whole, artistic activity in west Cornwall has at least a three-thousand-year history. The extraordinary presence of prehistoric standing stones and Celtic carvings, as well as indigenous craft traditions, have continued to influence art made in the region in the twentieth century.

In terms of modern art history, the first notable date is 1811, the year J.M.W. Turner visited the duchy. His sketches from this trip record Cornwall's natural beauty and romantic remoteness, and they inaugurate the dialogue between artist and landscape that dominates the later history of art in the region.

In the Victorian period, artistic activity in west Cornwall was bound up with wider social and economic developments. In the Midlands and the North the booming industrial towns provided education and employment for trained artists and designers. At the same time in Cornwall the traditional industries of fishing and tin-mining were in steep decline. The Great Western Railway arrived in St Ives in 1877, and the town's new accessibility brought a regular stream of visitors. New houses and hotels sprang up in the higher reaches surrounding the harbour, and between 1900 and 1920 St Ives gradually came to terms with its status as a resort and a working base for artists.

The first wave of artists to base themselves in St Ives came from more varied backgrounds than their Newlyn counterparts, and until the 1900s they tended to be summer migrants rather than permanent 'colonists'. An important figure was Julius Olsson, who was already a well-known artist before he settled in St Ives. In 1902 he began working in the Porthmeor Studios in old net lofts overlooking Porthmeor Beach where he also ran an 'atelier' style art school. St Ives's growing reputation made it, like Newlyn, a place for aspiring artists to visit early in their careers, and many, such as the Canadian Emily Carr or the Swedish artist Anders Zorn were from overseas. The town benefited from the fashionable appeal of artists' colonies in remote areas, combined with the availability of studio space and tuition. In addition, there were professional connections between artists in the teaching institutions in London and those in the art colonies. The early cosmopolitan mix of visitors to St Ives persisted throughout the colony's history. Between 1884 and 1920 prominent artists who visited Cornwall for varying lengths of time included J.A.M. Whistler, Walter Sickert, Frances Hodgkins, Matthew Smith and Cedric Morris.

J.M.W. Turner *St Ives* 1811 from the *Bude to Clovelly* sketchbook (TB CXXV A-49, Turner Bequest)

Matthew Smith
Cornish Church
1920

Cedric Morris
Frances Hodgkins
c.1917

A Vision of Simplicity 1920–1930: Leach, Nicholson, Wood and Wallis

Alfred Wallis *The Blue Ship* c.1934

While the early art colonists had been attracted to St Ives in pursuit of a general approach to painterly practice and a way of life, the town's significance in the 1920s can be related to two specific events. The first of these was the decision by Bernard Leach to establish a pottery there on his return to England from Japan in 1920.

Leach had trained as a painter and printmaker, but had discovered his vocation as a potter through contact in Japan with the oriental ceramic tradition. This he saw as combining the production of essentially functional objects with the potential for full artistic

and spiritual expression, achieved through the relationship between a pot's physical form and its decoration. Leach was invited by a wealthy patron to set up a pottery in St Ives. Here, initially with his friend and associate the great Japanese potter Shoji Hamada, he set about promoting his vision of the artist-craftsman. Over the years, Leach took on many local assistants as well as visiting students in his pottery. They became an important factor in drawing together the artistic life of St Ives with the wider local community. In 1927 Leach was a founder member of the St Ives Society of Artists.

The second formative event of the 1920s was the visit by the painters Ben Nicholson and Christopher

Wood to St Ives in August 1928, when they came across the 'naive' paintings of the retired seaman and marine rag-and-bone merchant Alfred Wallis. Nicholson later described how they 'passed an open door in Back Road West and through it saw some paintings of ships and houses on odd pieces of paper and cardboard nailed up all over the wall ... We knocked at the door and inside found Wallis'. Wallis's images, often painted on irregularly shaped pieces of old card, appeared childlike and incompetent by academic standards. Yet their freshness and immediacy had a strong appeal for more sophisticated artists who were striving for these qualities in their own work.

Wallis, a socially isolated and eccentric man, had taken up painting in old age and lived in near-poverty. He was lionised by artists and intellectuals in the wake of Nicholson and Wood's 'discovery' of him, and his paintings were avidly collected.

In various ways, therefore, during the 1920s St Ives can be seen as a place of pilgrimage for artists seeking renewal and a vision of simplicity that contrasted with the values of the metropolitan art world. In Nicholson's words, 'One was wanting to get right back to the beginning and then take one step forward at a time on a firm basis'.

Bernard Leach *Dish*
1929

Primitivism and Modern Art

There is a long European tradition of artists looking
outside the academic art world for means of expression that are simpler and more vigorous, fresher and
less calculated, than those allowed for by the reigning
artistic establishment of the day. This search has often
led artists to seek inspiration in the work of earlier
historical periods and also in the products of so-called
'primitive' cultures; the interest in African art in early
twentieth-century Paris is a good example.

In England a quest for a simpler or more 'real' way
of life found expression in the Victorian period in the
work of William Morris and the Arts and Crafts
movement. It was given new urgency in the decades
following the First World War when Europe seemed
to have lurched out of its old political and social
certainties. Bernard Leach's pottery may be seen as
the product of a search for simplicity and quality in
the production of pots. In English artistic circles
during this period (particularly the decade 1929–39)
the engagement with 'primitivism' manifested itself
in the high degree of interest excited by the work of
the St Ives artist Alfred Wallis.

Wallis, who came late to painting and had no formal
training, was by all accounts a strange and isolated
figure in the day-to-day life of his home town. After
Nicholson and Wood's 1928 visit he gradually
acquired iconic status as Britain's premier artistic
'primitive'; Nicholson spoke for many when he said
of Wallis's work: 'One finds the influences one is
looking for and I was certainly looking for that one'.

How Wallis felt about his fame, which brought him
attention but few material rewards, can only be
guessed. Indeed, the whole question of 'primitivism'
in modern art has unavoidable socio-political over-
tones. In retrospect, there are parallels between
Wallis' situation and that of the 'primitive' artists of,
for example, the European colonies in Africa. Where
the art-world cachet of such work did nothing to
ameliorate the oppression and exploitation endemic
in their daily lives, it is not clear whether Wallis's
evident enjoyment of his audience for his art
compensated for lack of material fulfilment.

Ben Nicholson and Alfred Wallis c.1940

Alfred Wallis *St Ives* c.1928

The Arrival of Modernism: the War Years 1939–1945

Important as they were in different ways, the busy artist's studios and the presence of Alfred Wallis in his Back Road West cottage and of Bernard Leach in his pottery on the town's western outskirts would not have been enough to turn St Ives into the centre of progressive contemporary European art that it became during the 1940s and the following decades. This was largely the result of a third formative event: at the onset of war in 1939 Ben Nicholson and Barbara Hepworth decided to move out of London for the safety of their young family and came to Cornwall at the invitation of a writer friend, Adrian Stokes.

During the 1930s the direction of Nicholson and Hepworth's work was similar. In painting and sculpture they were developing a vocabulary of pure, simplified forms, along with Henry Moore and such leading European practitioners of the new abstract art as Naum Gabo, Piet Mondrian, Constantin Brancusi and Jean Arp. For these artists abstraction and the concern with pure forms had a democratic, utopian social aspect and a universal character that could transcend national differences. This vision stood in stark contrast to the rise of fascism, with its emphasis on racial identity and literal, propagandistic art.

It should be remembered that, during the period up to the eve of the Second World War, Paris had remained the undisputed centre of the art world, and England, let alone Cornwall, was felt to be remote from the most progressive contemporary developments. In the late 1930s, however, many European artists and intellectuals emigrated to the relative safety of London; some, like Mondrian, were *en route* for America, others were attracted by the modernist outpost of St Ives.

Cornwall was to prove a fertile working environment for both Nicholson and Hepworth, and, alongside abstract themes, other concerns implicit in their work of the 1930s were to emerge more fully here. Hepworth had been exploring the modernist goal of 'truth to materials' and a refinement of natural forms in her carving of wood and stone. Nicholson's lifelong response to light as experienced in landscape can be seen even in his most severely abstract works. In St Ives they were joined by the sculptor Naum Gabo, whose work provided a crucial direct link to the heart of European modernism, raising awareness of art beyond the immediate locality. Younger artists such as Peter Lanyon, Wilhelmina Barns-Graham and John Wells responded to the modernist circle, though with limited opportunities to produce work during the war.

Unlike younger artists, Nicholson was not called up for active service; his writings during the war years helped publicise St Ives, and by 1945 the town's long-established status as an art colony had acquired a further dimension as an internationally known centre of modern art.

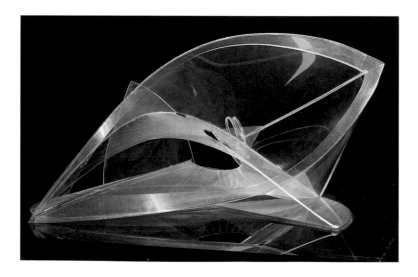

Naum Gabo *Spiral Theme* 1941

Above Ben Nicholson *June 1937 (painting)* 1937

Right Barbara Hepworth *Three Forms* 1934

Abstraction in Action

One of the central issues in modern art concerns the nature of abstraction. This question still stimulates passionate advocacy and violent hostility on all sides of the argument, even though the mid-twentieth-century heyday of 'abstract art' has now passed into history.

The term 'abstract' literally means 'separate' or 'apart'. In art it is often used as the opposite of 'figurative' to describe work that does not seek to portray something that the viewer can immediately recognise in the physical environment. Thus the sun can be shown in a figurative painting as circular and yellow, but a yellow circle on its own would be considered abstract – it could suggest many things to different viewers but does not obviously represent anything other than itself. Similarly, an unbroken blue horizontal line can suggest a horizon, but the viewer would need other clues – boats or wave forms, for example – to know for sure whether the painting was meant to represent the sea.

Western art in particular has been concerned with artists' abilities to create an illusion of real, three-dimensional forms in real space. In other traditions this is less important, and intricate decorative motifs, magical symbols and other non-representational images may be given far greater prominence than the attempt to create a replica of what we see around us. Whatever their approach to their work, artists themselves tend to be aware that the very act of creating an image involves a degree of abstraction – of making something that relates to, but is essentially separate from, the outside world.

St Ives is in many ways a very productive place to consider abstraction. In Barbara Hepworth's work, for example, the specific influence of landscape can be increasingly felt even in apparently abstract forms, and it is clear that a powerful consciousness of place played a vital part in her artistic development from the 1940s onwards. In the work of many other St Ives artists the influence of Cornish landscape and sea forms, colours and effects of light, as well as the region's history from its prehistoric megaliths to the tin-mining industry and its post-industrial legacy, can be traced in images that seem at first to be abstract.

Barbara Hepworth
Landscape Sculpture
1941

Terry Frost *Black and White
Movement* 1952

Abstract Variations on a Landscape Theme: 1945–c.1955

The period following the Second World War, up to 1956, is often characterised as the most dynamic and cohesive era in the development of modern art in St Ives. Its history is often told in terms of the different artistic personalities involved in the central debate of the time over the acceptance of abstract art.

From around 1943 Borlase Smart, a painter in the realist tradition who was nevertheless receptive to contemporary art advocated the inclusion of work by Hepworth, Nicholson and the new generation of modern artists in the exhibitions of the St Ives Society of Artists in the old Mariners' Church above the harbour. This arrangement proved unsatisfactory, and a group of younger artists, including Sven Berlin, Peter Lanyon, John Wells, Wilhelmina Barns-Graham, Bryan Wynter and the printer Guido Morris, began to organise separate displays in the church's crypt. By 1948 the so-called Crypt Group had grown to include among others David Haughton, Patrick Heron, Adrian Ryan and Kit Barker. In 1949 the Penwith Society of Arts was founded to provide a fresh arena

for modern art. This came to be understood by many as espousing an austerely abstract programme under Nicholson and Hepworth's influence.

The perceived polarisation of abstract versus realist art was felt by some artists to be too stark and unaccommodating. Peter Lanyon, in particular, advocated the need for modern artistic practice to embrace a greater plurality. He sought to promote the view that a locally based art could be both modern and international. Though abstract in the sense of not being literally representational, Lanyon's work explicitly handles landscape themes. His emphasis on a 'gestural' style of painting, in which individual brush marks are highly expressive, was shared by such contemporaries as Terry Frost and Patrick Heron. While owing a debt to modernism, it contrasts with the modernist emphasis on pure, sharply defined forms. Interestingly, a parallel development can be seen in Barbara Hepworth's sculpture of the late 1940s and 1950s, which makes more overt reference to the human form. An aspect of the new

Far left
Roger Hilton
February 1954
1954

Left
Peter Lanyon
Porthleven
1951

William Scott *Winter Still Life* 1956

world of the Welfare State is movingly documented in her hospital drawings of 1947–8.

Despite reservations, about both their influence on the Penwith Society of Artists and their tendency to dominate critical perception of St Ives art, Hepworth and Nicholson's example remained crucial. With their self-discipline and clarity of purpose, they exemplified serious, professional artists. Moreover, they provided direct support for many of the younger generation: Terry Frost, John Wells, Denis Mitchell, John Milne and many others worked for Hepworth as assistants.

In 1951 the Festival of Britain provided an opportunity for many of the artists associated with St Ives to make new works: Hepworth and Nicholson received major public commissions, and an Arts Council touring exhibition of large paintings included Peter Lanyon's *Porthleven* and Patrick Heron's *Christmas Eve* and *Blue Landscape*. In these works formal exploration of colour, space and line is combined with narrative or symbolic content. From the same period Terry Frost's work focused on more abstract concerns. Roger Hilton was closely in tune with new painting in continental Europe, and other artists who visited regularly at this time, including Alan Davie and William Scott, brought an awareness of American Abstract Expressionism. Patrick Heron's work as a critic during the 1940s and 1950s was important in highlighting new directions in British art and setting these in an international context.

Wilhelmina Barns-Graham *Red Form* 1954

23

Widening Horizons: c.1955–1964

While the leading figures of St Ives art in the 1940s and early 1950s can be viewed in the context of developments in and from European modernism, the focus in the later 1950s and 1960s shifted to new art movements in the USA. To some extent this reflects the fact that after the war New York rather than Paris became the capital of the international art world. An important date is 1956, the year of the exhibition *Modern Art in the United States* at the Tate Gallery in London. This brought a wider British public into contact with Abstract Expressionism, a movement in post-war American art that linked artists as diverse as Mark Rothko and Franz Kline with its emphasis on expressive spontaneity and emotional impact.

At the same time, it is true that European and British artists, including the younger St Ives artists, had helped to create the context for the positive reception, in New York as well as Britain, of the new American painting. Patrick Heron wrote of the charismatic confidence and individuality of the new American work, its sheer 'size, energy, originality, economy and inventive daring' and its radical 'denial of illusionistic depth'. And American audiences were also excited by contemporary British work: among the artists associated with St Ives who had solo exhibitions in New York and elsewhere can be listed Davie, Frost, Heron, Lanyon, Wells, Scott, Alexander Mackenzie, Paul Feiler and the sculptor Denis Mitchell.

Over this period many artists connected with St Ives had prominent roles in teaching institutions, for example Feiler at the West of England College of Art and Scott at the Bath Academy of Art. This stimulated wide-ranging contact between artists in Cornwall and elsewhere. Younger artists engaged in the new abstract art who were attracted to St Ives included Sandra Blow, Trevor Bell and Bob Law. In the international art scene St Ives art gained a reputation as a European form of abstraction which remained rooted in the observation of nature, in contrast to the contemporary tendency towards increasingly large-scale and uncompromisingly pure abstraction.

The notion of a close-knit, locally based artistic colony could by this time no longer be applied to St Ives. Some of the foremost 'St Ives artists', such as Frost and Hilton, frequently worked elsewhere, and the work of such artists as Lanyon, Heron and Wynter, who were more permanent residents in Cornwall, shows the pursuit of distinctive but not necessarily parallel aesthetic aims. The figurative work of Karl Weschke, Alan Lowndes and Patrick Hayman essentially stands outside the dialogue between abstraction and nature that forms the central concern of St Ives art from the 1940s on, yet they too could be considered as belonging to the wider context of modern art in Cornwall.

Tea at Chapel Kerris. Left to right, Meli Rothko, Mark Rothko, Terry Frost (hidden), Marie Miles, June Feiler, Helen Feiler, Christine Feiler, Anthony Feiler and Peter Lanyon.

Above left Patrick Heron
*Horizontal Stripe Painting:
November 1957–January
1958* 1957–8

Above right Bryan Wynter
Mars Ascends 1956

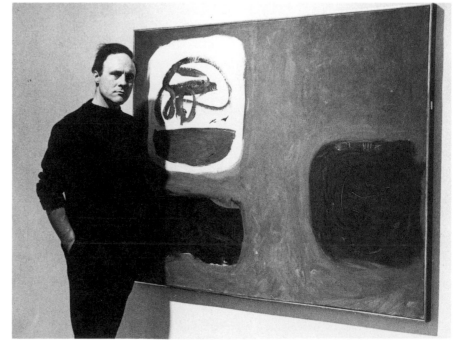

Patrick Heron at the
Bertha Schaefer Gallery
New York 1962

St Ives's International Affinities

St Ives is unique in British art history as a place that has given its name to a modern art movement. Its period of highest international profile was perhaps in the years 1956 to 1964, when many of the artists associated with the town were exhibiting in the USA and elsewhere abroad, but there had always been (and continues to be) a strong cosmopolitan element in the town's artistic life. Visitors to the Tate Gallery St Ives will notice that a high proportion of the artists shown in the main displays and featured in exhibitions either came from abroad or were exploring art styles that had originated far from the Cornish milieu.

The distinctive cosmopolitanism of St Ives art is an interesting phenomenon. Where else in Britain, outside London and other major cities, has a genuinely international artistic tradition flourished so long? West Cornwall and St Ives in particular have often been felt to be more Mediterranean than English in their climate and quality of light – the way the eye is constantly drawn towards and surprised by the sea, leaving all thoughts of 'mainland' England behind. This has certainly been a major feature in the area's attraction for very different kinds of artists.

So many wide-ranging international connections can be traced to and from St Ives over the years that there is room here to highlight only a few. In 1883–4, for example, in the earliest days of the St Ives art colony, the American-born painter J.A.M. Whistler spent a winter working in the town: his sketches show a profound response to the moods of light and cloud of the north-west sky facing Porthmeor Beach. Among the first young artists to come to study in St Ives were the New Zealand-born Frances Hodgkins and the Canadian Emily Carr. In 1920 Bernard Leach set up his pottery in St Ives after twelve years in Japan. He brought a highly personal vision of the meeting of Western and Eastern aesthetic and spiritual values embodied in the work of the artist-craftsman. Despite the fact that the area, with its dearth of suitable clays and of timber for kiln-firing, was not a promising location for a pottery, Leach found that his work and thought could thrive in Cornwall. The Leach Pottery became a place of pilgrimage for studio potters worldwide. In the 1940s the presence of Naum Gabo linked St Ives with mainstream European modernism, while Hepworth and Nicholson's fame made St Ives seem for a while the capital of British art. In the period since 1945 the growth of travel, communications and the increasing internationalisation – even globalisation – of the art world have been reflected in the hundreds of artists who have either settled or spent important phases of their careers in and around St Ives.

Bernard Leach at work in his studio

Patrick Heron *Azalea Garden: May 1956* 1956

Denis Mitchell *Turning Form* 1959

Experimentation and Diversity: 1964–1975

Peter Lanyon's death in 1964 as a result of a gliding accident has often been seen as symbolising the end of the great era of St Ives art. However, it is possible to see in Lanyon's very last works the emergence of new directions that were afterwards pursued by such painters as Bryan Wynter and Terry Frost (the so-called 'middle generation'). An example is Lanyon's use of fragments of real objects which he incorporated into his expressive brush marks, a development of his earlier practice of making three-dimensional models as 'working constructions' for his paintings. Echoes of this practice can be seen in the way Bryan Wynter used found objects and pieces of cut-out coloured card to translate his floating coloured brush marks into three-dimensional kinetic works called

'IMOOS' (Images Moving Out Onto Space). Terry Frost experimented with hanging objects, collaged elements and painted sculpture from the late 1950s onwards.

Works of this kind relate the St Ives artists to a widespread exploration of unconventional media in the mid-1960s. An important difference, however, was that the St Ives work continued to refer back to painting. Wynter is a good example of this: his kinetic works began as a way of extending a painter's perception of nature and later came to assist him in distilling nature back into two-dimensional form. The beauty of St Ives played a part in publicising the art with which it was associated. The writings of Denys Val Baker, for example, drew attention to the

Right Terry Frost *Through Blacks* 1969

Peter Lanyon *Lost Mine* 1959

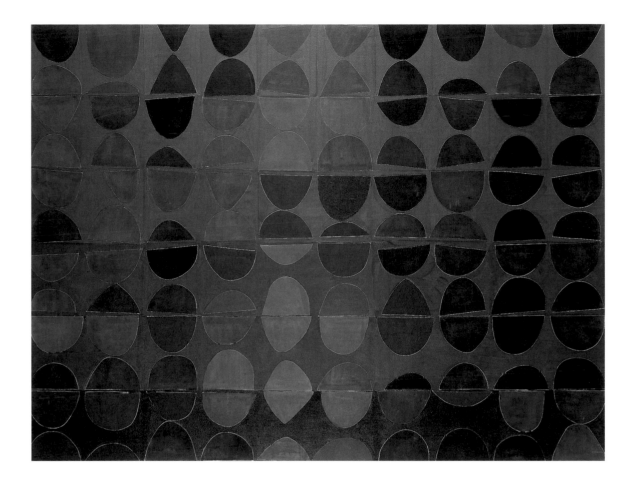

relationship between new art in Cornwall and the unique Cornish heritage and landscape.

From the 1960s onwards, however, it becomes increasingly difficult to associate St Ives with a particular style of art. Since that time hundreds of artists making very diverse work have spent time in west Cornwall. The contacts made in the USA by Heron, Scott, Lanyon and others brought American visitors including Mark Rothko and the critic Clement Greenberg, while a counter-current gave rise to a rejection of the dominance of American art and its critical perceptions. An important development of the later 1960s centred on younger artists and critics who saw in the flat expanses of American painting the final phase of all possible evolution of that medium. Many of these turned to the possibilities of Conceptual Art, with its exploration of other modes of communication such as photography, text and video, and its emphasis on the ideas presented rather than on the traditional process of artistic creation. This is now evident in the new projects presented at Tate Gallery St Ives.

Bryan Wynter *Imoos VI* 1965

Continuing Traditions and New Directions

In the 1980s St Ives art was celebrated by two important exhibitions in England (at the Tate Gallery in 1985) and Japan (a touring exhibition in 1989), in both of which the final date was taken as 1975, the year that saw the deaths of Barbara Hepworth, Roger Hilton and Bryan Wynter. But many St Ives artists, including Terry Frost, Wilhelmina Barns-Graham, Denis Mitchell, Paul Feiler, John Wells and Patrick Heron, continued to live and work in west Cornwall. Some work remained firmly based in the locality, including the remarkable images of Bryan Pearce, while other artists moved on after a fruitful period in the area, a notable example being the Irish artist Tony O'Malley, who returned to Ireland after two decades in Cornwall. Since 1993, some artists have chosen to return to St Ives., including some, like Sandra Blow and Trevor Bell, who spent time in St Ives earlier in their careers.

Today many younger artists work in west Cornwall. Some are directly associated with the leading St Ives figures of older generations, some simply have a new commitment to living and working in the region alongside new groups and in partnership with new galleries.

In the context of both St Ives' rich artistic tradition and the diversity of contemporary artistic practice in west Cornwall, the role of the Tate Gallery St Ives embraces a wide range of different activities. The Gallery actively builds on its presentations of the Tate's collection of modern art in Cornwall, through new acquisitions and by stimulating responses to the displays through its Education and Projects programmes. Special exhibitions provide an opportunity to highlight the work of an individual artist or group of artists, while an artist-in-residence scheme allows the Gallery to promote and often commission new works of contemporary art conceived in relation to the St Ives context. The Gallery's work includes projects with younger artists and with visitors to the region; collaborations with public galleries elsewhere in the UK and abroad; and major regional projects such as the St Ives International which brings a renewed emphasis to Cornwall's place in the international art world. Through a combination of all these activities, Tate Gallery St Ives aims to present a picture of art in the region which highlights both its rich and diverse history, and the continuation of this legacy through new developments in contemporary art.

Opposite, above Bryan Pearce *St Ives from the Cemetery* 1975
Opposite Terry Frost *R. B. and W. Spiral for A.* 1991
Left Karl Weschke *Body on the Beach* 1977

Public Galleries in Cornwall

While the displays at the Tate Gallery St Ives offer a broad and varied overview of St Ives art, individual artists are also represented by important works in public collections elsewhere, including the Tate Gallery in London. Art created in or associated with Cornwall can also be seen at other galleries and museums in Cornwall.

Newlyn Art Gallery first opened in 1895 as a showcase for painting of the Newlyn School. It now runs a varied programme of contemporary art exhibitions, including work by nationally and internationally important contemporary artists and regular exhibitions by members of the Newlyn Society of Artists.

The Royal Cornwall Museum houses a fine permanent collection of paintings including work by Robert Opie, Julius Olsson, Borlase Smart and Lamorna Birch. It also stages regular exhibitions of contemporary art.

Penzance and District Museum and Art Gallery is home to a major collecton of Newlyn school painting, including work by Norman Garstin, Stanhope Forbes and Laura Knight.

Falmouth Art Gallery and Museum houses a fine collection of Cornish marine painting and also stages exhibitions of contemporary art and crafts.

© 1997 Tate Gallery All rights reserved
Published by Tate Gallery Publishing Ltd
Millbank, London SW1P 4RG

Edited by Michael Bird based on text by Michael Tooby from *Tate St Ives: An Illustrated Companion*

Designed by James Shurmer
Printed in England by Beacon Press, Uckfield

Front cover: Tate Gallery St Ives from Porthmeor Beach
Back cover: Terry Frost *Black and White Movement* 1952

Tate Gallery St Ives Information

Tate Gallery St Ives
Porthmeor Beach
St Ives TR26 1TG
Tel: 01736 796226

Barbara Hepworth Museum and Garden
Barnoon Hill
St Ives TR18 1AD
Tel: 01736 796226

Opening Hours
1 April–30 September: daily 11a.m.–7p.m.
1 October–31 March: Tuesday–Sunday 11a.m–5p.m
Opening hours may may be subject to change. Please telephone before you come.

Tate Friends St Ives
Joining the Friends gives you special access to the Tate through member-only previews and events all the year round. It enables you to make an important contribution to the Tate Gallery St Ives by supporting a wide range of projects, educational programmes and the purchase of works of art. To join, phone the Tate Gallery Membership Office on 0171 887 8752.